Utopia
Liberty & Capitalism

How to Create an Ideal Society

Written and Narrated by Alexander Calarizien

Published by Calarizien Publishing, LLC
a Calarizien® Company

First Edition: 2025

eBook ISBN: 979-8-9931289-0-0
Audiobook ISBN: 979-8-9931289-1-7
Hardcover ISBN: 979-8-9931289-2-4
Paperback ISBN: 979-8-9931289-3-1

Library of Congress Control Number: 2025947367
Publication City: Las Cruces, New Mexico

www.UtopiaLibertyandCapitalism.com

Knowledge is Power

CALARIZIEN

Prologue

This work is titled "Utopia" as coined by Sir Thomas More in 1516, is used to describe a society that does not exist but has the possibility to exist as a type of unachievable goal, the ideal society. The following pages describe the ideas and structure required to build the ideal nation using the knowledge we have learned and presented in a direct, to-the-point format, designed to be read in a couple of hours, and easily referenced.

Preamble

Why I'm writing this book:

Latin phrase "Nemo vir est qui mundum non reddat meliorem" in English "What man is a man who does not make the world better"

"We should not be like children with their parents, simply accepting what we are told" Marcus Aurelius

The role of government is to defend the rights of its citizens, provide administrative structure, and collect taxes to provide law and order, defense from foreign threats, education, infrastructure, and encourage the expansion of knowledge and understanding of its people.

If you are looking for more detail and examples not provided in this writing, I direct you to the Holy Bible.

Table of Contents

Definitions

Definitions are provided to clarify the purpose of selected words. Clear communication must come before ideas may be shared and understood.

- Right – Moral, Inherent, and Legal Entitlement of a Human
- Freedom – Ability to pursue your own happiness without interference from others
- Religion – Philosophical belief held by an individual or group of individuals
- People / Person / Individual – Human with different legal classifications listed below
    - Adult – Person of legal age who is fully grown and developed with a sound mind
    - Citizen – Adult member of Utopia with the right to vote, own land and/or permanent property, keep and carry weapons, own and operate a business
    - Resident – Adult who is allowed to live, work, and operate a business in Utopia but does not have the rights of a citizen
    - Visitor – Adult who is allowed to visit Utopia for a defined period and does not have the rights of a citizen or resident

    - Dependent – Underage (child), Disabled (mentally, of any age), or Elderly Dependent (old age) who are the responsibility of an Adult (Citizen, Resident, or Visitor)
- Government / Nation / State – Legal entity whose duty is to protect its people by enforcing and maintaining the rights and laws of its citizens
    - Federal – Highest level of government, government of the nation
    - Regional – Middle level of government, government of a defined area within the nation, usually determined by a geographical area of similarity (Plain, Coastline, Mountains, etc.)
    - Local – Smallest level of government, government of a defined city within a Region
- Soldier – Citizen employed to provide security to the people by serving the federal government in combat and/or preparation for combat against a foreign entity
- Law Enforcement – Citizen employed by the government to enforce the laws of the nation

- Laws – Set of written codes all must obey or suffer consequences from the government as the enforcer of laws on behalf of the people
- Crime – Violation of the Nations Laws (which includes the Rights of the People)
- Property – Describable item of value owned by a person(s) (private property) or the government (public property)
    - Land – Defined surface area (land above or below water) within the nation, could be owned by a Citizen or Federal/Regional/Local government
        - Productive Food Land – Land used for growing crops and/or raising of livestock for food production (must be in use/producing food at expected rate)
    - Permanent Property – Structure on land with design and purpose to be permanent
    - Personal Property – Possessions owned that are not Land or Permanent Property
    - Public Property – Land, Permanent Property, and Personal Property, owned by a government entity
- Land Value – Value of the Land without Permanent or Personal Property

- Infrastructure – Structure and facilities needed for the operation of society (roads, railroads, power stations, water treatment, sewer, trash, airports, etc.)
- Company / Business – Legal entity created and maintained for business purposes, can be a responsible entity if not owned by a Citizen or Resident of Utopia
    - Responsible Entity – Business operating in Utopia but not owned by a Citizen or Resident. Therefore, it requires a legal entity of responsibility (not a human).
- Free Market – economic system where prices and goods are determined by the free choice of the market participants (buyers and sellers)

Individual Rights

The rights of the individual are the first place to start when creating an ideal society, as individuals are the building blocks of a society. The individual must be protected both in health and in possessions and have the liberty to seek out their own success or failure at their own will.

The goal of an ideal society is to provide the individual with as much liberty as possible.

By protecting individual freedom and ensuring that the individual has the most freedom possible, a nation no longer needs to have protected groups, as the individual is the smallest possible group, and the only one that needs defending.

United States Bill of Rights, Ratified December 15, 1791

1. Congress shall make no law respecting an establishment of religion, or prohibiting the free exercise thereof; or abridging the freedom of speech, or of the press, or the right of the people peaceably to assemble, and to petition the Government for a redress of grievances.

2. A well-regulated militia, being necessary to the security of a free State, the right of the people to keep and bear arms, shall not be infringed.

3. No soldier shall, in time of peace be quartered in any house, without the consent of the owner, nor in time of war, but in a manner to be prescribed by law.

4. The right of the people to be secure in their persons, houses, papers, and effects, against unreasonable searches and seizures, shall not be violated, and no Warrants shall issue, but upon probable cause, supported by oath or affirmation, and particularly describing the place to be searched, and the persons or things to be seized.

5. No person shall be held to answer for a capital, or otherwise infamous crime, unless on a presentment or indictment of a Grand Jury, except in cases arising in the land or naval forces, or in the Militia, when in actual service in time of War or public danger; nor shall any person be subject for the same offense to be twice put in jeopardy of life or limb; nor shall be compelled in any criminal case to be a witness against

himself, nor be deprived of life, liberty, or property, without due process of law; nor shall private property be taken for public use without just compensation.

6. In all criminal prosecutions, the accused shall enjoy the right to a speedy and public trial, by an impartial jury of the State and district wherein the crime shall have been committed, which district shall have been previously ascertained by law, and to be informed of the nature and cause of the accusation; to be confronted with the witnesses against him, to have compulsory process for obtaining witnesses in his favor, and to have the assistance of counsel for his defense.

7. In suits at common law, where the value in controversy shall exceed twenty dollars, the right of trial by jury shall be preserved, and no fact tried by a jury shall be otherwise re-examined in any court of the United States, then according to the rules of the common law.

8. Excessive bail shall not be required nor excessive fines imposed, nor cruel and unusual punishments inflicted.

9. The enumeration in the Constitution, of certain rights, shall not be construed to deny or disparage others retained by the people.

10. The powers not delegated to the United States by the Constitution, nor prohibited by it to the States, are reserved to the States respectively, or to the people.

Summary of the Rights granted to the Citizens of the United States in the "Bill of Rights":

1. Freedom of Religion and its Practice
2. Freedom of Speech
3. Freedom of the Press
4. Freedom to Peacefully Assemble
5. Freedom to Petition the Government
6. Freedom to Keep and Carry Weapons
7. Freedom to Deny Entry to your Home
8. Right to be Secure in Ones Possessions and their Privacy
9. Right to be Judged by One's Peers is All Serious Legal Cases
10. Right to a Speedy and Public Trial
11. Right to be Tried Only Once
12. Right to Reasonable Fines and Bail Without Cruel or Unusual Punishment

13. Rights not Listed in the Constitution are Not therefore Denied by the Constitution
14. Authorities not Granted or Prohibited by the Constitution belong to the State or People

Additional Rights later added to the United States Constitution:

15. All People Born or Naturalized in the United States are Citizens
16. No State may Make or Enforce any Law which Violates the Rights of its Citizens
17. No State may Deprive any Person of Life, Liberty, or Property without Due Process of Law
18. All People are Guaranteed Equal Protection Under the Law
19. All Citizens have the Right to Vote

Additional Rights of Citizens from Nations Outside of the United States:

20. Right to Healthcare
21. Right to Education
22. Right to Gender Equality
23. Right to Housing

24. Right to Life Worthy of Human Beings including Social Welfare and Employment Support
25. Right to Strike and Collective Bargaining (labor union protections)
26. Right to Privacy
27. Freedom from Double Taxation Abroad

The rights of citizens or people within a nation must not conflict with themselves or other rights. For example, a citizen cannot have the right to the labor of another citizen (Healthcare), nor could a citizen have the right to a possession that must be earned or produced by another citizen (Housing). The rights of Utopia are designed to provide the maximum liberty to every citizen.

Utopia – Individual Rights (Cannot Violate Laws of the Nation)

1. Freedom of Yourself to Make Your Own Choices including Life, Death, and Health, of Yourself (Adult Only)

2. Freedom to Practice Religion of Choice (Adult Only)

3. Freedom to Raise Children as Their Parent(s)/Guardian(s) Choose (Adult Only)

4. Freedom of Speech, Press, Publication, Expression, Art, Social Media, and Privacy

5. Freedom to Assemble and Use Public Land and Public Property

6. Freedom to Own, Hold, Maintain, and Develop, Land and Permanent Property (Citizen Only)

7. Freedom to Buy, Own, Use, and Sell, Weapons Equal to that of Military Personnel (Citizen Only)

8. Freedom to Defend Yourself and Others and the Property of Yourself and Others

9. Freedom to Defend Yourself Against the Government if Accused of Violating a Law

10. Freedom of Innocence Until Proven Guilty by a Court of Law in Utopia and Granted a Speedy, Public Trial, that may Only Occur Once

Government Structure

The government should be structured in such a way that it serves the people of the nation but does not rule over them. The government must be limited in its power, to only what is needed.

"Laissez-faire capitalism" is the economic philosophy of free-market capitalism that opposes government intervention. The theory of Laissez-faire was developed by the French in the 1700's and proposes that economic success is more likely the less government is involved in business.

Each aspect of the economy, which is essentially roles in society (farming, medicine, construction, transportation, banking, etc.), inherently have their own experts and best practices. It is highly unlikely that any single individual would or could understand every aspect of the economy (including members of leadership). Therefore, any regulations imposed should be designed and implemented by experts in that field/aspect of the economy, and with input and majority consent of those being regulated. The goal of any regulations imposed should be the fair and honest desire for equality of opportunity, and prevention of systemic, field wide failure (mass starvation, sustained power outage, or banking system collapse, etc.).

No person or entity should be entitled to anything beyond what they themselves have earned or received freely from another. It is up to each person with the rights they inherently possess (Utopia – Individual Rights) to think, work, and earn, what they have or have not.

The government (Federal, each Region, each Local) should have a single leader. This single leader system provides clarity, efficiency, vision, and sole responsibility. The most successful leaders have chosen a council of advisors to help guide and administer their responsibilities (Alexander the Great had the Companions "Hetairoi", Louis XIV the Royal Council, King David and Charlemagne their Advisors). Leaders must serve their people with the trust and respect of the people, "When the people fear their government, there is tyranny; when the government fears the people, there is liberty" Thomas Jefferson.

Each level of government should have the responsibility and power to govern their portions of society. For example, the federal government should negotiate international relations and not one of the regional or local governments. The federal/national government should be responsible for the national policy and only national policy, the region for the region, and the local for the local. Every government policy and decision should be publicly available and include who made the policy/decision and if it was a vote, who voted for or against the decision.

The federal government should provide the required administrative systems for all government-related processes within the nation. All processes should be digital and as automated as possible, to provide the greatest service to the people, at the least cost. For example, issuance of passports, birth and death records, transfer or purchase of land and/or permanent property, should all be carried out by the people requesting/submitting the documentation and automated through an online federal system.

Federal Responsibility

- Enforcement of Federal Laws
- Issue Currency
- Collect Federal Taxes (Sales Tax and Tariffs/Import Tax)
- Federal Planning
- National Infrastructure (Power Plants, National Roads/Freeways, National Parks)
- Law Enforcement (Escalation/Support of Regional and Local Law Enforcement)
- National Defense
- International Relations
- International Trade Regulations including Tariffs
- Education (Curriculum, Testing, Accreditation, Funding)
- Scientific Research (Space Exploration, Weapons Development, Medical Research, Digital Security)
- Recordkeeping & Property Register (People Records, Education, Government Employment, Crime, Land Ownership, Land Value, Productive Food Land, Permanent Property, Taxes, Companies, Trademarks, Copyrights, Patents)

- Security and Secrecy of (technological developments, scientific understanding, military capabilities, government records, and personal information of the people)
- Banking and Trade Regulations for a Free Market

Regional Responsibility

- Law Enforcement (Escalation/Support of Local Law Enforcement)
- Collect Regional Tax (Land Value Tax)
- Regional Planning (With Guidance from Federal Planning)
- Regional Infrastructure (Dams, Airports, Regional Roads)

Local Responsibility

- Law Enforcement
- Law Violation Punishment
- Collect Local Tax (Land Value Tax)
- Local Planning (With Guidance from Federal and Regional Planning)
- Local Infrastructure (Government Offices/Courts, Parks, Local Roads)

Taxes

Adam Smith who wrote An Inquiry into the Nature and Causes of the Wealth of Nations and is commonly considered to be "The Father of Modern Economics", proposed the idea of the Invisible Hand, was a proponent of Laissez-faire economic policies, and argued that Free Trade/Markets tend to regulate themselves by means of competition, supply and demand, and self-interest.

Adam Smith's Principles of a Fair Tax:

1. The subjects of every state ought to contribute towards the support of the government, as nearly as possible, in proportion to their respective abilities; that is, in proportion to the revenue which they respectively enjoy under the protection of the state.

2. The tax which each individual is bound to pay ought to be certain, and not arbitrary.

3. Every tax ought to be levied at the time, or in the manner, in which it is most likely to be convenient for the contributor to pay it.

4. Every tax ought to be so contrived as both to take out and to keep out of the pockets of the people as little as possible over and above what it brings into the public treasury of the state.

Summary of the Principles of a Fair Tax:

1. Ability to Pay, in Proportion to Available Revenue

2. Certain, Not Arbitrary

3. Convenient to Calculate and Pay

4. Efficient in Supporting the State

The United States tax code does not as of the year 2025 meet any of these principles, nor the tax codes of any other developed nations. To follow the principles of a "Fair" tax and to provide the government with the revenue necessary to operate but not rule over its citizens, the following tax policies are proposed.

Though it would seem a good idea for land that is owned by citizens to never be taxed, this does not work, as the land of a nation belongs to the citizens of that nation and to encourage growth and use of the land, owners should be taxed a small portion of the land value, on a regular basis, to ensure they are economically incentivized to use the land or allow someone else to purchase and use the land.

1. Each level of government should have its own clear and certain tax and should be responsible for the collection of its tax (No Other Taxes).
   - Federal/National Tax – Sales Tax on Finished Goods and Tariffs on Imported Goods
     - Percentage determined by Federal Government
     - No Sales Tax on Land or Permanent Property (as they are not consumed but later resold, again and again, taxation would also interfere with this market)
     - Recommendation – less than 15%
       - recommendation provided as guidance for size of government
     - Tariffs used for international relations/negotiation
   - Regional Tax – Land Value Tax
     - Percentage determined by Regional Government

        - Lower rate for productive food land
    - Land Value determined by Regional Government with guidance framework provided by Federal Government
    - Recommendation – less than 3% of value and less than 1% of value of productive food land
        - recommendation provided as guidance for size of government
- Local/City Tax – Land Value Tax
    - Percentage determined by Local Government
    - Land Value determined by Regional Government
    - Recommendation – less than 4% of value and less than 2% of value of productive food land
        - recommendation provided as guidance for size of government

2. Every person who is conducting business (citizen, resident, visitor, dependent, responsible entity) in the county should

contribute to the support of the government "Pay Tax".

3. Taxes should only be levied once, no "double" taxation. For example, only the sale of the finished goods/products should be taxed and not during the stages of production.

4. Import taxes "Tariffs" should only be levied on nations who levy a tax on our nation "Utopia" and should reflect the levied tax (to make the taxes levied between the nations in effect equal). Free and open trade between nations with no taxes, fees, or barriers, is the goal of international economic policy.

5. All taxes should be collected by the governing entity that is imposing the tax and should be done when they are levied (sales tax) or on a regular basis so as not to create large periodic payments (recommendation – Land Value Taxes paid monthly).

6. Medical/Healthcare should be completely privatized, the suggestion that medical services could be a right is morally wrong, as that would in effect give one group of people (non-

healthcare workers) the right to the labor of another group of people (healthcare workers).

7. Taxes used for infrastructure projects should be funded by a single government source, for example the federal government should be responsible for the national roads that span the nation, but the local roads should be maintained by the local government. Each type of infrastructure should be determined as Federal, Regional, or Local, so responsibility for its development and/or maintenance is clear.

Law & Order

The government should, on behalf of the people, enforce the Rights of Citizens and Laws of the Nation. The first successful laws of a nation are the Ten Commandments which serve as a basis for law today.

The Ten Commandments from the Holy Bible, first in the King James Version "KJV" and then in the New International Version "NIV".

> KJV - Thou shalt have no other gods before me.
> NIV - You shall have no other gods before me.
>
> KJV - Thou shalt not make unto thee any graven image, or any likeness of anything that is in heaven above, or that is in the earth beneath, or that is in the water under the earth.
> NIV - You shall not make for yourself an idol in the form of anything.
>
> KJV - Thou shalt not take the name of the Lord thy God in Vain.
> NIV - You shall not misuse the name of the Lord your God.
>
> KJV - Remember the sabbath day, to keep it holy.

NIV - Remember the Sabbath day by keeping it holy.

KJV - Honour thy father and thy mother, that thy days may be long upon the land which the Lord thy God giveth thee.
NIV - Honour your father and your mother.

KJV - Thou shalt not kill.
NIV - You shall not murder.

KJV - Thou shalt not commit adultery.
NIV - You shall not commit adultery.

KJV - Thou shalt not steal.
NIV - You shall not steal.

KJV - Thou shalt not bear false witness against thy neighbour.
NIV - You shall not give false testimony against your neighbor.

KJV - Thou shalt not covet thy neighbour's house, thou shalt not covet thy neighbour's wife, nor his manservant, nor his maidservant, nor his ox, nor his ass, nor any thing that is thy neighbour's.
NIV - You shall not covet.

The laws of a nation should be clear and concise, so they may be understood and obeyed by all. Violation of a nation's laws should also have clear consequences to help prevent the violation and provide expectation and understanding of the consequences. The laws of a nation include the rights of the people provided in the Individual Rights chapter. For a crime to occur there must be a victim, therefore if there is no victim then the person was exercising their own freedom, for example you cannot be your own victim.

Punishment for crime (violation of the nation's laws) should provide greater loss to the criminal, than to the victim. If a person steals from another person, then the stolen property should be returned to the original owner, along with a fine paid by the criminal to the state, for the cost of their prosecution (the criminal pays more than they took, justice requires punishment). If a victim cannot be returned what they lost, such as in the case of physical violence, then the criminal should be punished in a way to offset the crime.

Only accused people shall be physically held by a government entity in a jail/prison until guilt or innocence is determined. All accusations, evidence, court proceedings, and punishments, should be available to the people unless it could cause harm to the victim. If the accused is found innocent, then the alleged victim may be accused of violating the rights of the originally accused.

Using jail/prison time as punishment for a crime is ineffective, as it does not provide a return to the victim or to the state, and adds to the costs of the people (including the victim) to house, feed, and confine the criminal. When a crime cannot be repaid with money, such as the case with physical violence, or the criminal does not possess the required money, then the state should punish the criminal in a way that benefits the aggrieved person and community. Punishments may include fines, labor provided to the state, physical violence onto the criminal, and in the case of heinous crime, such as murder, the criminal should be executed as they are unfit for society.

Utopia Laws (Cannot Violate Individual Rights)

1. Shall Not Violate the Individual Rights of Another

2. Shall Obey Adult Parent(s)/Guardian(s) if a Child/Dependent

3. Shall Not Murder or Physically Harm Others

4. Shall Not Steal

5. Shall Not Lie Under Oath

6. Shall Not Harm Public Property or the Property of Others

7. Shall Not Violate the Practices of the Government, Must Pay Taxes

8. Land of the Nation Belongs to the Citizens, Private Property Belongs to Citizen(s) for Their Use, Public Property Belongs to All Citizens (with reasonable restrictions for safety and security)

9. Only Citizens May Own Land or Permanent Property in the Nation

10. Only Citizens May Serve in a Public Capacity (Government, Military, Education, Law, or Scientific Research Funded by the Government)

Military & International Relations

Maintaining a strong miliary, foreign intelligence, and international relations service, is important to protect the Rights of the People, and Laws of the Nation.

The military should be organized and professional, under the command of the Federal Government. The military is only to be used against foreign opponents and never against the people of the nation. As the goal of the military is to protect the people of the nation, it should limit its interference in conflicts between other nations and people, unless they pose a direct threat to the people of Utopia.

To protect the people of the nation and their property, it is necessary to have a secure border (the ability to admit those who should enter and repel those who shouldn't enter). As the border serves as the legal and many times physical walls of a nation, against foreign interests, it should be protected by the military of the nation and enforced with all available military resources, equipment, and tactics.

All military personnel must be citizens of the nation or providing their service to the nation, as part of their requirement for citizenship (citizenship requires military service). The service required for citizenship should not be longer than one year, and the personal weapons issued to the military service members (soldiers) will belong to the soldier after their service is complete, for them to use and possess. This requirement for citizenship ensures that all citizens have a vested interest in the nation, are capable of aiding in the defense of the nation, the nation has enough active military personnel, and each citizen of the nation can defend themselves.

International Relations is the responsibility of the Federal Government, and should focus on protecting the Rights, Laws, Property, and Interests, of its people. To develop respect and not resentment from other nations, the negotiations and tariffs enacted should be equal to those of the opposing side. For example, if another nation has 10% tariffs on Utopia, then Utopia should have 10% tariffs on the other nation. Only in times of War, should the equal (eye for eye) goal be abandoned, and a policy of complete domination adopted.

Foreign Intelligence is the responsibility of the Federal Government, and provides information to help guide the military and international relations. As this information may be critical to the defense of the nation, a foreign intelligence service should be well funded and utilize the latest available technology.

Education

Education or the lack thereof drives the capability of a nation, as it drives the capabilities of each individual citizen and resident. Education is an important component of knowledge and "Knowledge is Power" (Calarizien motto). Though education cannot be a right, as it requires the labor of another person, it is advantageous to have a highly educated population. To build the ideal society, that continues to grow and expand humanity's capability and understanding, education should be supported and funded by the Federal Government (people of the nation) to ensure all the people of the nation have access to education.

Utilizing free market capitalism in education will facilitate more efficiency, better results, and more choices for parents and students. Therefore, all education should be privatized with the Federal Government providing funding for each student to attend the school of their choice (parents' choice in case of a dependent). All funding should be of the same amount, for each student, at the same level of study. For example, the funding for a child in a first-grade class (introduction to reading and mathematics) should be the same amount as every other child studying first grade, and the same funding for an individual studying aerospace engineering, should be the same for all aerospace engineering students.

Parents and students should have the free choice to choose which school they and/or their child attend. With the school receiving funding from the federal government for each student in attendance, they are incentivized to have more students. Competition between schools will lead to better education, that is more tailored to individual preferences. For example, some schools may focus heavily on sports and have robust physical education training facilities, while another school may focus on science and have sophisticated science labs.

As education will be part of the free market, some schools may choose to cater to wealthier individuals and ask students to pay a premium above the federal government funding. At the same time, some schools may focus on providing education with all meals and time for activities included, with long operating hours to match the work schedule of their students' parents and do so at the federal government funded rate. While other schools, may focus on test scores or other measurable results to help students' admission into top tier programs and job opportunities.

All schools should utilize the latest technology, which currently provides near instantaneous sharing of information. For example, all lessons/lectures should be available in audio and video, from multiple sources, with ratings from students and teachers, allowing the best and most engaging lectures to rise to the top. This way students can choose their favorite lecturer or approach (visual, audio, text, or hands-on) that best suits them. Through free-market competition, and the use of newer technologies, new learning and teaching techniques will emerge over time, and increase the overall understanding of the population.

All levels of education should be funded by the federal government, so long as it provides increased capabilities for society. For example, if a student wishes to pursue mathematics, the federal government should provide the funding to a school until the student achieves the highest level of mathematical education possible, decides to stop the schooling at a level they are happy with, or is unable to complete the requirements and must stop at the level they achieved. When government funding for education is not provided, society suffers. In many developed nations, such the United States, where higher education is not provided, the best and brightest citizens are effectively punished with crushing student debt, for their attempt to better themselves and succeed in life.

Testing will be required for all students to pass each level of education and move onto the next one. The tests should be created by education experts, funded by the federal government, and administered for each subject, at each level, for each student. The tests should include both the remembering/memorizing of information and the understanding/impact of the information. Only if a student passes the test of a subject, are they allowed to move on to the next level of that subject. The government will only fund the education of each level once more, after the student fails to pass the test at that level. If the student is a child, the government will continue to fund the education of the student.

Children are the responsibility of their parents and therefore their parents have legal rights over them. The goal of society is for parents to care for and teach their children as best they can, so that they may learn and grow. The Individual Rights and Laws of the Nation apply to All (including children) so though a parent has the right to raise a child as they see fit, they are not allowed to harm the child (common discipline tools such as spanking, that do not cause lasting damage, excluded). Only if a child is born with major mental or physical defects, to the extent that their life would be a burden upon their parents and society, are they to be euthanized, or if an individual chooses not to be a parent the unborn child aborted. If a child does not have parents or a guardian who is willing to take responsibility for them, then the child will become the responsibility of the state, and will attend a school that provides year-round education, food, clothing, and shelter (boarding school). Only if a child is acknowledged by its parent/parents is a parent responsible for the child, and the child a dependent of that parent/parents (no forced parent(s)/guardian(s)).

Military training will be part of the educational curriculum offered to students to ensure a strong nation, and population capable of defending themselves and others. All students should learn military tactics and weapons training in school, so they are prepared to provide short term voluntary military service to Utopia (as part of the requirements to become a citizen of Utopia). Over time, this training and service will cause the majority of the population to be ready to serve the country in time of war and/or disaster, both of which are less likely the stronger the population of a nation becomes.

To become a citizen of Utopia, an individual must complete a level of education that demonstrates their ability to contribute to the nation, by possessing the basic knowledge for a productive life, complete the required minimal military training and service, and swear an oath to Utopia that they will defend the rights and laws of the citizens and nation. If a person does not complete the requirements to become a citizen, then they will become and remain a resident, until the requirements are completed.

Science & Technology

The Federal Government should fund scientific research and development, for the purpose of advancing human understanding, technological progress, and military capabilities of the nation. The advancements gained through this research and development, belong to the citizens of the nation, and should be shared with them whenever possible (excluding only, what is currently or expected to be used for national defense).

Funding should be focused on development and research, with full and complete documentation of all learnings, designs, results, specifications, etc., integrated into a digital design and research program, that can be used and expanded upon by other researchers, not just the company that received the initial funding. The funding process should be setup as to fund a lot of work in different ways, rather than completing one large project. For example, instead of funding one huge project to build a rocket to another star, break apart each of the different milestones required and learn from the results. This will maximize ideas and alternative processes through competition and lead to the best result in the shortest time, such as a rocket to another star.

Military weapons funding should be focused on research and development, with mass manufacturing planned, tested, and ready, but the nation should only produce what the military is currently needing/could use in the first few weeks of a conflict (minimal stockpiling). When mass military equipment is needed, such as in a time of war, the nation could produce the newest and best equipment for the conflict, as it has been focusing on creating better equipment and learning, rather than producing what would become outdated and unused. For example, drones are quickly taking the place of soldiers in battle as they can fly, carry heavier weapons, and are much more disposable. Therefore, drones should be under constant development, with companies innovating designs and constantly creating newer better versions. This way, when a conflict occurs the nation could mass-manufacture the newest and best drones, as one of the weapon systems that overwhelm the opponent and help end the conflict.

Using the best information, systems, and processes available is advantageous to society, both in the present and especially the future. For example, the Metric system is far superior to the older Imperial system and should be adapted as the standard system until a better system is developed (society should not hold onto the past with respect to technological understanding and adaptation). Another example is the tracking of time, Zulu Time "Military Time" (a fixed time, on a 24-hour clock, irrespective of location) is far more efficient and easier to use than the time zone system (currently used by most countries). Currently, the United States has adopted and even worse time system, combining the time zones system, with "Daylight Savings" time, which changes time nonuniformly twice a year.

History of Successful Societies

When designing our ideal society of Utopia, it is important to learn from the successful societies of history, in addition to our current societal successes and failures. All successful societies of the past had a single cultural identity and genetic similarity (of the same tribe). From ancient Egypt, Greece, and Rome, to the Germanic nations of Europe, who conquered and colonized most of the world, to the Asian societies of Japan and China, who have held global importance for millennia, by maintaining a cohesive culture and homogeneous population.

From the single Aryan group of humans who originated in Europe (not to be confused with the ideological use of the word in the early to mid-1900's; "Aryan" in this work is used to describe the historical peoples of Europe, who created "Western Civilization" culture and society) multiple Aryan branches have had great success during periods of social cohesion and tribal unity. The Hellenic branch of the Aryan's was the first to emerge as a dominant society (ancient Greece). The ideals of free will and being a "free people", were first used to great success within city-states, who used scientific study to expand technology and created the field of philosophy. At its height the Hellenic people conquered the then known world, under Alexander the Great.

The Italic branch of Aryans, who arguably created one of the greatest nations in history (Rome) built and maintained their vast empire by initially, only allowing the Italic tribal members to hold public office and serve in the military. One of the causes of Rome's eventual collapse was the use of non-romans in the military during the Imperial period, who inevitably betrayed the Romans and sacked Rome itself, leading to the end of the Western Roman Empire and the Rome we commonly associate with.

The Celtic peoples were a branch of the Aryans, who expanded and populated most of western Europe during the time of the Romans. Unfortunately for the Celts, they were not able to form larger societies, and their individual tribes remained small and rife with inner tribal conflict (failure to choose a single leader/king of their people). This failure to form cohesion throughout their people and unite when attacked, led to their defeat by the Germanic tribes, who overtime conquered and assimilated the other branches of the Aryans, following their sack of Rome.

The Germanic branch of the Aryans expanded out of Central Europe with many tribes forming new nations, such as the Angles/Saxons/Jutes » England, Franks » France, Visigoths » Spain, Norse » Norway, Sweden, Denmark, and many other nations across the continent. Though the Germanic tribes conquered the continent of Europe, they adapted a Feudal system of government and economic policy, which led to stagnation and wars of inner family conflict. Over time commerce began to expand through a restricted but slowing emerging rebirth of capitalism (Capitalism being the only naturally occurring and inevitable economic form). Liberties were also slowly expanded and added into laws, from the Magna Carta to the Constitutions of new republican states, which provided rights to citizens.

As the Aryan nations of Europe grew stronger through liberty and capitalism, their populations and influence began to expand. Though some nations had elected leaders, many of the European nations still had kings (from the Feudal system), who provided the nation, a single leader, with defined powers. The European military power, technology, societal unity, and size, made them unstoppable opponents to most other societies at the time, which led to the Europeans conquering and colonizing most of the world. This

European world dominance continued until the nations of Europe and their allies fought each other in WW1 and WW2. Since WW2, the nations of Europe have been in decline, as their populations continue to lose societal cohesion, individual liberty, and free capitalism.

Utopia Requirements for a Successful Society
The Rule of One

- One People/Tribe (Unified by Language, Culture, & Religion)

- One Set of Rights and Laws (Defined & Understood by All)

- One Leader (Defined Power Who Governs by Consent of the People)

Conclusion

All is a work in progress, and nothing is finished. To create the ideal society, we must take what we have learned and expand upon it. Rights only exist so long as people are willing to fight for them, and tyranny is the inevitable outcome of apathy.

"The Truth is like a lion; you don't have to defend it. Let it loose, it will defend itself." Augustine of Hippo

Freedom is a universal human desire and Liberty is the expression of that freedom within a society, guaranteed with Individual Rights. "Give me liberty or give me death!" Patrick Henry

"Capitalism is the only system in history where wealth is not acquired by looting, but by production, not by force, but by trade, the only system that stands for man's right to his own mind, to his work, to his life, to his happiness, to himself." Ayn Rand

"Fortune Favors the Bold" Alexander the Great

Utopia Individual Rights
(Cannot Violate Utopia Laws)

1. Freedom of Yourself to Make Your Own Choices including Life, Death, and Health, of Yourself (Adult Only)

2. Freedom to Practice Religion of Choice (Adult Only)

3. Freedom to Raise Children as Their Parent(s)/Guardian(s) Choose (Adult Only)

4. Freedom of Speech, Press, Publication, Expression, Art, Social Media, and Privacy

5. Freedom to Assemble and Use Public Land and Public Property

6. Freedom to Own, Hold, Maintain, and Develop, Land and Permanent Property (Citizen Only)

7. Freedom to Buy, Own, Use, and Sell, Weapons Equal to that of Military Personnel (Citizen Only)

8. Freedom to Defend Yourself and Others and the Property of Yourself and Others

9. Freedom to Defend Yourself Against the Government if Accused of Violating a Law

10. Freedom of Innocence Until Proven Guilty by a Court of Law in Utopia and Granted a Speedy, Public Trial, that may Only Occur Once

Utopia Laws

(Cannot Violate Utopia Individual Rights)

1. Shall Not Violate the Individual Rights of Another

2. Shall Obey Adult Parent(s)/Guardian(s) if a Child/Dependent

3. Shall Not Murder or Physically Harm Others

4. Shall Not Steal

5. Shall Not Lie Under Oath

6. Shall Not Harm Public Property or the Property of Others

7. Shall Not Violate the Practices of the Government, Must Pay Taxes

8. Land of the Nation Belongs to the Citizens, Private Property Belongs to Citizen(s) for Their Use, Public Property Belongs to All Citizens (with reasonable restrictions for safety and security)

9. Only Citizens May Own Land or Permanent Property in the Nation

10. Only Citizens May Serve in a Public Capacity (Government, Military, Education, Law, or Scientific Research Funded by the Government)

Love God

Protect Your Family

Fight For Your People

Made in the USA
Coppell, TX
14 January 2026

65728637R00036